Dr. Funster's
QUICK THINKS MATH C1

Fun Math Brain Teasers

Titles in this series
Quick Thinks Math A1
Quick Thinks Math B1
Quick Thinks Math C1

Robert Femiano

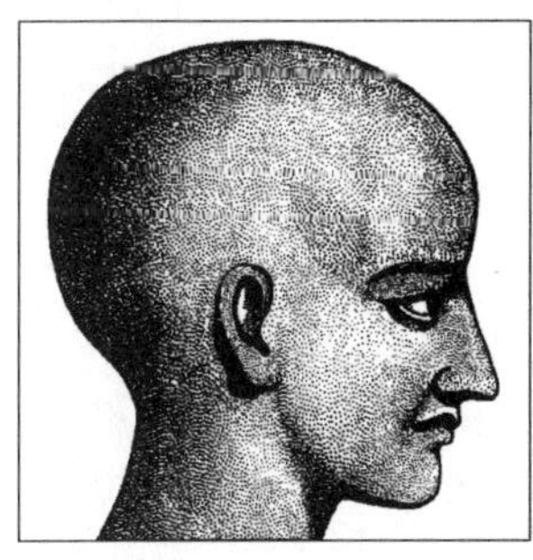

CRITICAL THINKING BOOKS & SOFTWARE
www.CriticalThinking.com
P.O. Box 448 • Pacific Grove • CA 93950-0448
Phone 800-458-4849
ISBN 0-89455-831-5
Printed in the United States of America

About Dr. Funster's QUICK THINKS MATH

Objective

Quick Thinks Math problems were designed to introduce and reinforce mathematical concepts in a quick, fun way. The activities emphasize logic and reasoning skills needed to build a strong foundation in mathematics.

Skill Level

Quick Thinks Math problems are thinking activities and need only elementary math skills to solve. Problems in Book C1 are arranged according to degree of difficulty—from easier problems in the beginning to more difficult problems towards the end. Book C1 is suitable for grades 8-10 and requires a working knowledge of multiplication and division. The focus of Book C1 is on place value, scientific notation, ratios, and higher-order reasoning skills.

Teaching Suggestions

Ask students to explain their answers both orally and in writing. Most of these problems can be solved in more than one way. Plenty of space has been provided between the problems to encourage students to write everything down, step by step. This process will strengthen thinking and math-communication skills.

Emphasize the importance of going through all the steps. The process of problem solving is often more important than the answer. When students are having difficulty, focus their attention on what they already know about the problem and what they need to find out.

Dr. Funster's Series Titles

Think-A-Minutes A1, A2, B1, B2, C1, C2

Word Benders A1, B1, C1

Visual Mind Benders A1, B1, C1

Creative Thinking Puzzlers A1, B1, C1

Quick Thinks Math A1, B1, C1

STUDENT TIPS FOR PROBLEM SOLVING

1. Do you know what the problem is asking you to find? (What do you need to know to give the answer?) You may need to read the problem 3 or 4 times—Don't panic!

2. Do you expect the answer to be larger or smaller than the largest number in the problem? About how much do you think the answer should be? (This is called estimating the answer.)

3. Put small numbers in place of large numbers, and then read the problem again.

4. Draw or act out the problem.

5. Guess and check.

6. Make a chart or table.

7. Work the problem out backwards.

8. Read the problem again. Plug in information that you've already solved.

9. Try using blocks or other things to help you "see" the problem.

10. Does your answer make sense? Did you put your answer back in the problem and read it again?

1. What fraction is exactly halfway between 1/100 and 1/1000?

2. Is anyone more than a billion seconds old? (calculator time!)

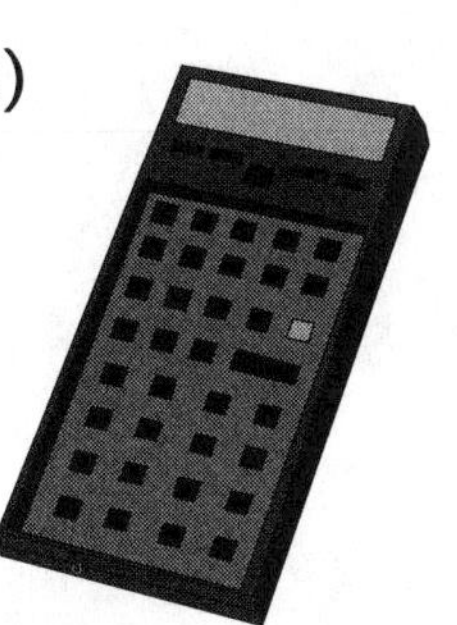

3. What number am I? Take 3/5 of me and you'll have my reciprocal, 5/3.

4. Quick! How many zeros are in one zillion?

a. thousand billion
b. 1000 x 1000 x 1000 x 1000
c. thousand million
d. none of the above

5. What 3 numbers, 1 apart from each other, sum to 5?

6. A clerk opened the cash register and found that she could give more than a dollar in change but could not give exact change for a dollar. What is the greatest number of coins the clerk could have without having exact change for $1?

7. A shoebox measures one-half foot by one-half foot by one foot. How many shoeboxes can be packed into a cardboard cube that measures 3 feet in each direction?

8. A refrigerator cools 2 1/4 degrees every hour and a half. If the temperature is 48 degrees at noon, what time will it reach 38 1/2?

9. There are 12 ways to make a quarter without using a quarter. So how many ways would there be to equal 50¢ without using a quarter or a half dollar?

10. What is the sum of the first 1000 numbers? Does it help to pair up the 1 with 999 and the 2 with 998 and so on?

11. Rachel will triple her age in 36 years. How old is she now?

12. What is .01% of an hour?

13. Ramona's classroom plant grew .021 meters in one day. She noticed that the plant's height had quadrupled. How tall is the plant now?

14. Dominic is twenty-five years old and shares the same birthday with his sister, Margo, who is eighteen. At what age was Dominic three times older than his sister?

15. A pizza that measures 14 inches across the center is approximately how much larger than a 10-inch pizza?

a. 50%

b. 75%

c. 40%

d. 100%

e. 150%

16. Robert sells four-legged and three-legged stools. He sells 4 four-legged stools for every 3 three-legged ones. If he has 1000 stool legs, how many three-legged stools should he build?

17. A student noticed that she was 1/3 done with her math problems and that after doing 6 more, she'd be halfway done. What problem number did she just finish?

18. If 4% of a number is 3, what fraction of the number would 25 be?

19. Six brothers, each born 2 years apart, have a total age of 198. How old is the oldest?

20. Two friends in different towns begin walking toward each other. One walks 1/2 mile in 24 minutes while the other walks the same distance in 20 minutes. If they meet 2 1/2 hours later, how far apart are the towns?

21. The 25 first graders had the difficult job of sharing 2 dozen doughnuts. What percent of a whole doughnut does each student receive?

22. What number completes the pattern:

10%, 11.11%, 12.5%, 14.28%, ____, 20%
(Hint: Think outside of percents)

23. Which is a better deal:

a. an item reduced by 15% with an additional 15% taken off that reduced price

b. 30% off the full price

24. A game spinner has three colors. Red is twice as likely to be spun as white while blue is twice as likely to come up as red. So what fraction of the spinner is white?

25. Find the values of A and C in this series:

__A__, __B__, 64, 80, 144, 400, __C__

26. The Moon is approximately a quarter of a million miles away from Earth. The Sun is 36,500% farther. If light travels at 186,000 miles each second, how long does it take sunlight to reach us?

27. Find the value of C such that all numbers are equidistant.

0.1, __A__, __B__, __C__, 1.1

28. Each of the scales below is in balance. Find the missing number.

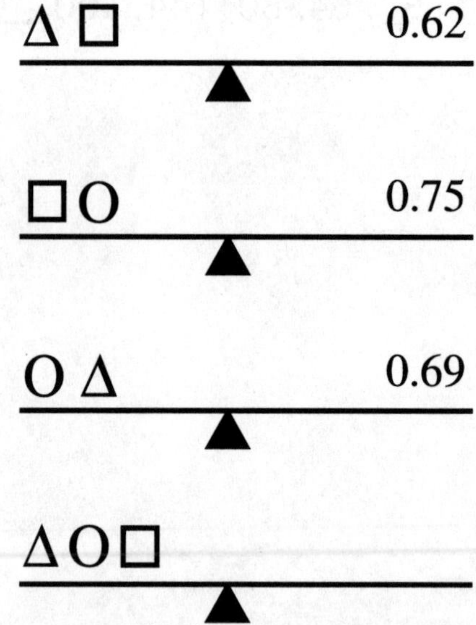

29. In your head, find the sum of 11.11 + 22.22 + ... 99.99 and round it to the nearest one.

30. A farmer has 2 cows for every 5 chickens in her barn. If she counts 198 legs, how many animals are in the barn?

31. A father gave his son 5/7 of his monthly allowance, keeping the rest for a previous debt. The son spent 5/7 of what his father gave him, and now has $9.60 left. What is the son's normal allowance?

32. Ellen had 5 coins. She gave 2 to her brother, but she still had twice as much money as he did. What is the most amount of money she could have for this to be true? How many of the 19 ways can you find to answer this? (Use any current American coins.)

33. In these triangles, the bottom numbers are used to make the top number. The same mathematical procedure occurs in each triangle. Find the missing number.

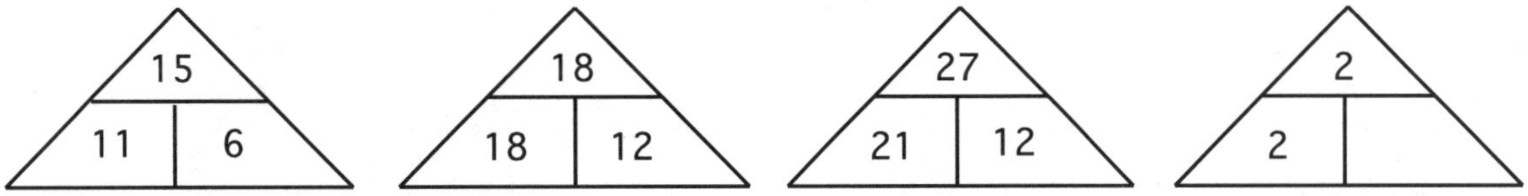

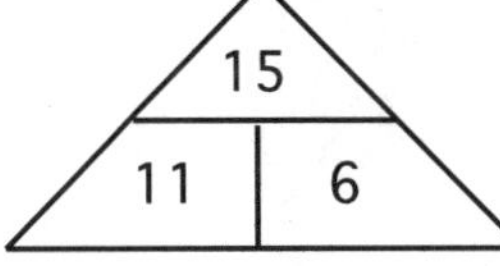

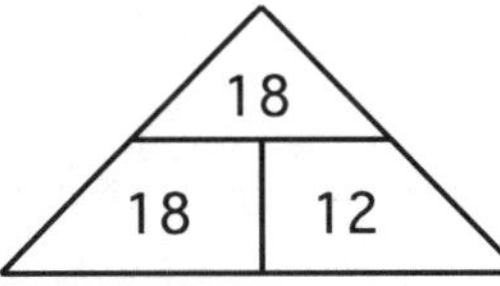

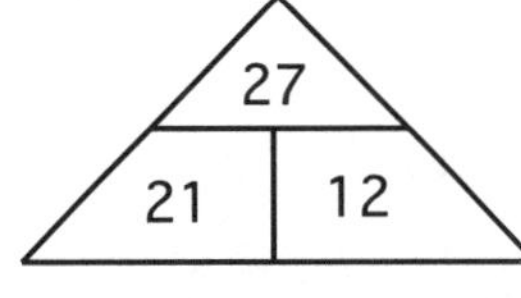

2
2

34. Brian wakes up at 6:24 A.M. and wonders what fraction of the day he has slept.

35. I have 2002 thousands in me and my digits add to 10. If no digit is used more than twice, what is the smallest number I can be?

36. One day, an elementary school principal noticed the following: At 12:05 P.M., all the students in his school were eating in the lunchroom; but at 12:15, only 4/5 of them were still there eating. Ten minutes later, 1/8 of the remaining students left for recess. At 12:35, three times as many students then left as had left by 12:15. If there are now only 19 students in the cafeteria, how many students attend the school?

37. Use parentheses and add whole number operation signs in the □ to make this statement true.

$$1 \square 2 \square 3 \square 4 = 6$$

38. One trillion dimes would be how many quarters?

39. When writing the numbers from 0 to 10,000, how many 9's will you write? Remember that it takes 2 nines to write 99.

40. Quick, in your head, what is half of nine hundred ninety nine million, nine hundred ninety nine thousand, nine hundred ninety nine?

41. One more in your head: A treasury mint stamps out ten million quarters every day. If you could have 0.1% of this, how many dollars would you have?

42. A pizza company puts pepperoni on every 6th pizza it makes, olives on every 8th pizza and mushrooms on every 10th pizza. How many pizzas will they have to make to end up with 10 that have all 3 toppings on them?

43. The students of Denny Middle School had a car wash fundraiser. They charged $6.50 for a basic wash and $9.50 for a deluxe wash/wax. If they sold 8 basic car washes for every 3 deluxe, how many cars did they wash if they earned $322.00?

44. What two evenly spaced numbers will complete this pattern:

1 1/3, ____, ____, 3

45. In this problem, all scales are balanced. Find the value of each shape.

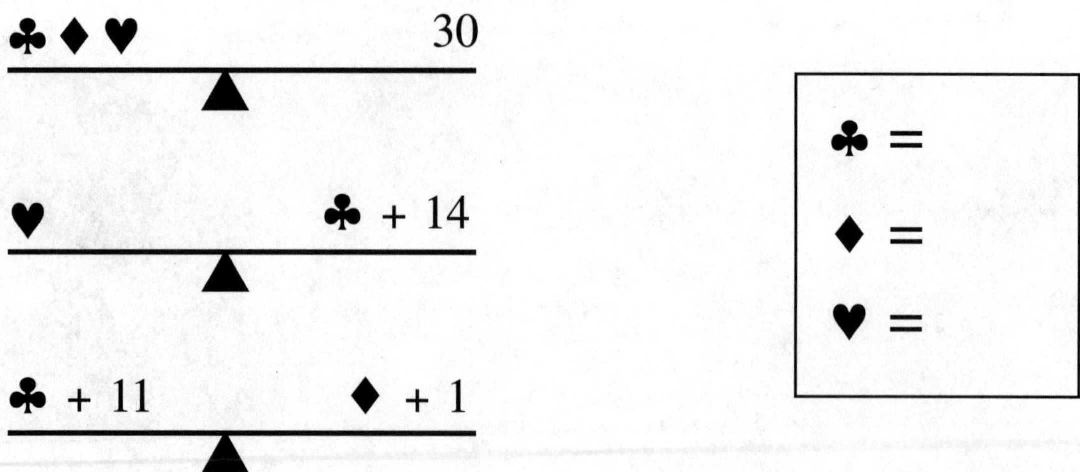

46. Will a half-billion pennies make you a millionaire?

47. Suppose Margaret used two different rain gauges to measure the amount of rain from an overnight storm. In one, she found 2/3 of an inch; in the other, she collected 3/4 of an inch. What fraction of 3/4 of an inch does the 2/3 of an inch represent?

48. What point on the number line is 17/18 of the distance between .01 and .10?

49. For each problem, use the addition, subtraction, multiplication and division symbols once each to make the equation true.

a. 600 □ 200 □ 400 □ 300 □ 200 = 200

b. 200 □ 300 □ 600 □ 400 □ 200 = 200

50. Balance the last scale using one of the lettered choices.

O Δ — θθ

θ — ΔΔ

ΔΔ — □

OO —

a. □□

b. Δ□O

c. □□Δ

d. □O

e. □O□

51. Balance the last scale using one of the lettered choices.

O♣ — ♥

□♣ — Δ

OΔ —

a. ♥

b. ♣□

c. □♥

d. □□

e. ♣♥

52. Use 4 different even numbers, from 4 to 14, to fill in the blanks.

___ years ago, Margo was 7 years old because last year she was ___ years old, and next year she will be ___. In ___ years, she will be 23.

53. Use just these numbers to make a sum of 100. You can use a number more than once.

16, 17, 23, 24, 29, 39

54. Mr. Femiano is twice as old as his son. Next year he will be 31 years older than his son. How old is his son?

55. Find 2 numbers that are 13 times the sum of their digits.

56. Willy is twice as old as Katrina. Twenty-seven years ago Katrina was 2/5 of her current age. So how old is Willy?

57. Use the numbers 1 to 6 to make this equation true.

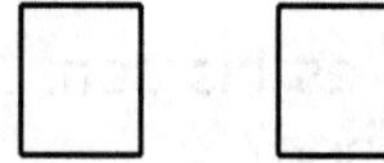

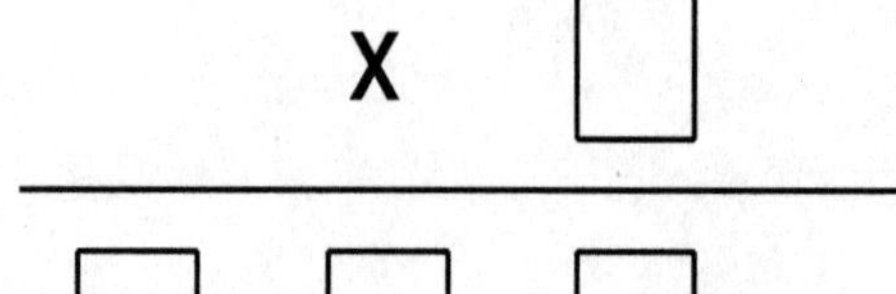

58. Ellen buys 3 six-packs of juice, then buys one additional bottle. If a six-pack is exactly $3.00 more than a single juice and the total was $15.00, how much did the single bottle cost?

59. Who am I? My 4 different digits sum to an even number. My hundredths digit is the smallest, and it is odd. My tenths digit is twice my thousandths digit. I have fewer ones than thousandths. My first two digits, together, are evenly divisible by my last two digits together.

60. With the eastern morning sunlight warming his kitchen, Robert noticed that the temperature steadily increased 7/8 of a degree every 3 minutes and 7 1/2 seconds. The temperature has doubled twice since sunrise at 6:15:30 A.M., and it is now 52 1/2 degrees warmer. What time is it?

61. Three dads and three sons want to cross a river. Each knows how to row a boat, but the boat holds only two children or one adult. If the river is one mile wide, how far will they have to row the boat for all the people to cross the river?

62. What number am I? I am a number close to 10,000. You hear me when you count by 10's, 30's, and 45's.

63. How many numbers between 0 and 1000 have more tens than ones?

64. How many numbers between 0 and 1000 have the same number of ones and tens?

65. What number belongs in space A?

__A__, __B__, 10, 1000, 1,000,000, 10,000,000,000

66. If the average weight of 4 people is 150 pounds and the average weight of two of them is 75 pounds, what is the average weight of the remaining two people?

67. If a hiker went from base camp to summit and back in 20 hours, and the ascension was at 2 kilometers per hour while the climb down was at 3 kilometers per hour, how far is it from base camp to peak?

68. If □□□□□□□□□ = 3 then □□□ = ____

69. If you added up the numbers from 0 to 50, would the answer be even or odd?

70. A 10¢ gumball machine holds two types of gumballs: sour and sweet. There are twice as many sweet types as sour. Sours include the same number of lemons as limes but half as many grapefruit. There are two sweet flavors: cherry and strawberry. There are four times as many cherries as strawberries. What percent chance does someone have of spending 30¢ and receiving a strawberry gumball?

71. Two numbers add up to 605. One of the numbers is divisible by 10, and the result is the second number. What are the two numbers?

72. A man is 140% of his son's weight. Together they weigh 360 pounds. What is the difference in their weights?

73. A basketball is dropped from the top of a tall building to the flat sidewalk below. It falls 1920 inches and, after the third bounce, reaches the height of 240 inches. The height the ball reaches after each bounce is always the same fraction of the previous bounce. What is this fraction?

74. Julie gave $10 to Jane and Jane gave $8 to Gia. At that point, Julie had $10 more than Jane and $20 more than Gia. Before she gave away her money, how much more did Julie have than Jane and Gia?

75. The sum of each row is given to the right. Replace the question mark with a shape to complete the equation.

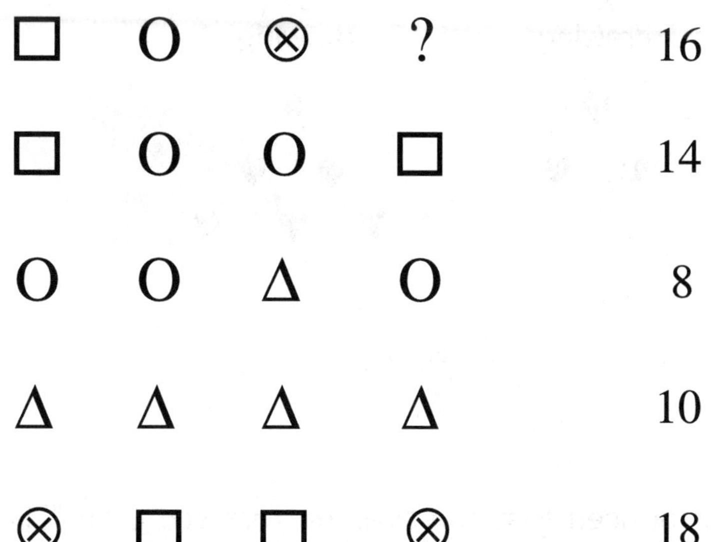

76. Two identical boxes have three identical books in them. If the total weight is 1.1 kilograms and the books are 4 1/2 times the weight of the box, how much does one book weigh?

77. A painter is standing on the middle rung of her ladder. She goes up three rungs, then down five and then back up six more. She is now 2/3 of the way up. How many rungs does the ladder have?

78. How many hearts will be in the 100th drawing?

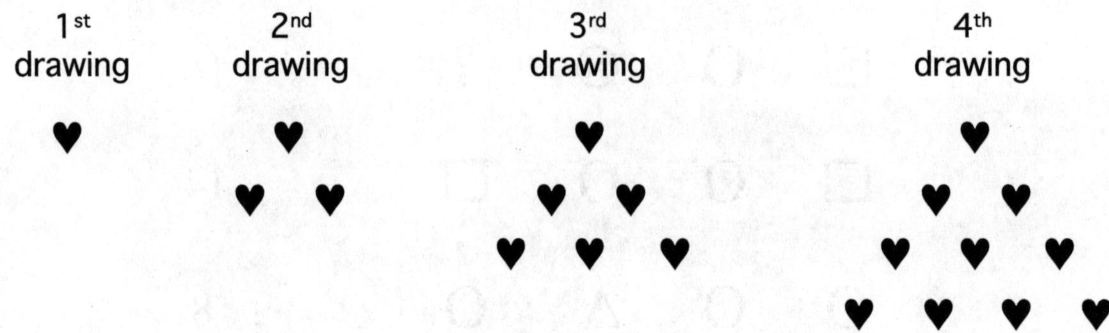

79. A teacher noticed that the average test score on "Finding Averages" was 84% for her class of 20. She also noticed that when one paper was not included, the average rose to 85%. What was the score of the missing paper?

80. If you played this game, would you win money or lose money? Six cards, labeled 0–5, are shuffled and turned face down on a table. You may turn over any two cards. If they sum to 3 you win $7 but if they don't, you owe $1. Explain your reasoning.

81. A teacher said, "In my hand are coins, none worth more than a quarter. All but 6 are pennies. All but 6 are nickels. All but 6 are dimes, and all but 6 are quarters. How much money do I have?"

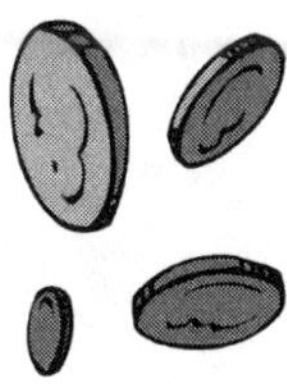

82. One number is 4 times another number yet their sum is –1. What is their difference?

83. The sum of 2 numbers is 2 and the difference is 1. What is their product?

84. A number series goes as follows: –2, 3, 8, 13 ... What is the 101st number?

85. If you were to continue this chart, in which row and column would you place the number 1,000,000?

	A	B	C	D	E	F
Row 1	1	2	3	4	5	6
Row 2	7	8	9	10	11	12
Row 3	13	14	15			

86. A beginning painter can apply one coat of paint to a house in 36 hours, and a journeyman painter can do it in 28 hours. If they work together for 8-hour days, starting at 8 A.M. on Monday, at what time and day will they finish applying one coat each? Do not consider lunch or other breaks in time.

87. The following square is a Magic Square in which the rows, columns and diagonals all total the same. The "magic" sum is 1. What is the value of A?

.452	O	G	H
.209	E	.398	F
C	.425	.101	D
.049	B	A	.371

88. Kerri has 62.5% of the money her cousin Ashley has. What percent of money does Ashley have compared to Kerri?

89. Using only a single digit greater than 2, along with addition signs, make an equation totaling 1000. Bonus: Find two answers.

For example, 222 + 222 + 222+ 222 + 22 + 22 +...2 = 1000

90. Five students want to have dinner for under $60, including the 10% tax and 15% tip on the whole bill. What is the most they can spend on dinner to come in under their budget?

91. Claire spent all of her money on 5 rides at the amusement park. As she stepped up to each ride, she paid $1 more than half of what she had in her pocket. How much did she start with before the first ride?

92. What is the sum of all the digits needed to write the numbers from zero to one thousand?

93. Dom is having dinner with a friend, Craig. He bought 5 dishes while Craig bought 3. At the last minute, a third friend comes and equally shares from all the dishes. All the dishes cost the same. The last-minute friend paid $1 for each dish, which was his share. What amount should Dom and Craig each pay?

94. A feed and seed store owner buys 100-pound bags of grass seed and wants to make a 70% profit by reselling the seed in 10-pound bags. Unfortunately he ends up making only a 60% profit. He figures his scale must be in error. Therefore, when his scale says 1 pound, how much does the seed truly weigh?

95. Mr. Jones lives in Jonesville. There are four roads out of Jonesville, each leading to Thomasville. From Thomasville, there are three roads, each leading to Clarksville. How many different ways can Mr. Jones commute to Clarksville and back while going through Thomasville, and not repeating any routes?

96. These scales are balanced. Replace the ? with one of the choices.

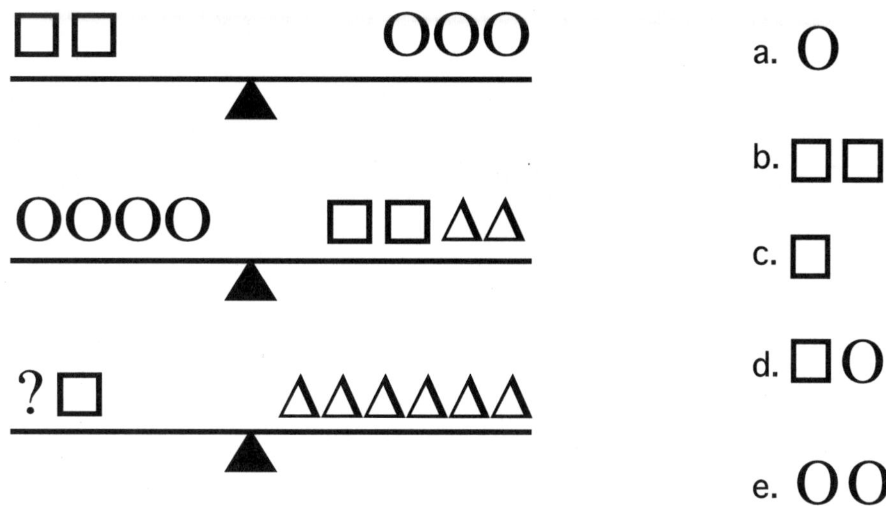

97. In these triangles, the bottom numbers are used to make the top number. The same mathematical procedure occurs in each triangle. Find the missing number.

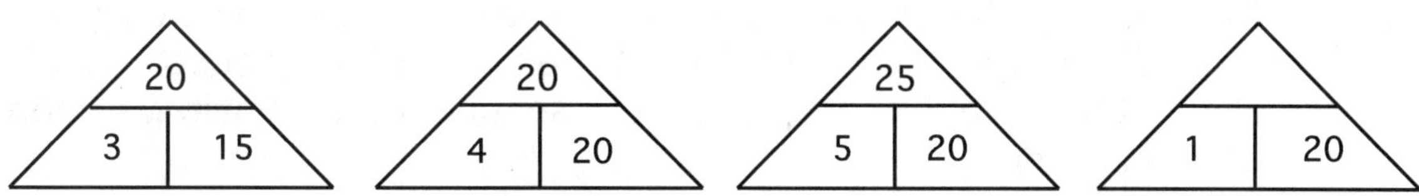

98. If the volume of a cube is 512 cubic inches, how far is it from the very center to the top corner (to the nearest 1/4 inch)?

99. A record company charges $28 for a double CD set. This price has a 40% profit built in. Employees can buy the same CD for 15% under the company's cost. What would an employee pay?

100. Movie A plays in three theaters for two weeks, five times daily. Meanwhile, Movie B plays for three weeks in two theaters, four times daily. During that time, 66,000 people went to see Movie B and 80,000 people saw Movie A. If all theaters have the same amount of seating, which movie was more popular each showing?

101. An airplane propeller measures 2.5 feet from the center to the tip. If it revolves 1320 times per minute, how many miles will the tip travel in one hour? A mile is 5280 feet.

102. A sports team is owned equally by three men and two women. One man sells half of his shares to the other men. Later, one of the other two men sells half of his shares to one woman while the last man sells 3/5 of his shares to the other woman, with one receiving twice as much as the other. What proportion of the team do the women now own?

103. 75% of 88 is the same as 55% of what number?

104. How many solid cubes, with total surface areas of 150 square centimeters, will it take to make a larger cube with a total surface area of 3750 sq. cm.?

105. In this number sequence, the first two numbers are 1 and 3. The third number is 4 and is formed by adding the previous two numbers. If this rule is followed, how many of the first 100 numbers will be odd?

ANSWERS

1. **11/2000**. 1/100 = 100/10000 and 1/1000 = 10/10000. The difference between these fractions is 90/10000, half of which is 45/10000. Add this to the 10/10000 making the midpoint at 55/10000 or 11/2000.

2. **Yes**. Anyone who is more than 31 3/4 years old. One year has 31,536,000 seconds. Dividing that number into 1 billion gives the answer.

3. **2 7/9.** If you know what 3/5 of a number is, then you can find 1/5 of the same number by taking a third of this. Then 1/3 of 5/3 is 5/9, which represents one of the five parts. 5 x 5/9 gives the secret number.

4. **d.** There is no such number as zillion.

5. **2/3, 1 2/3, 2 2/3.**

6. **11 coins.** She could have 3 quarters, 4 dimes, and 4 pennies.

7. **108.** The cardboard box is 27 cubic feet. It takes 4 shoeboxes to make one cubic foot, so 4 x 27 = 108. *OR* 18 shoeboxes can be packed on the bottom layer, which is 6 inches deep. Then, you will have 6 layers for a total of 108.

8. **6:20 p.m.** It cools 1/4 degree every 10 minutes (90 minutes divided by 9/4 degrees). To cool 9 1/2 degrees will take 380 minutes (9 1/2 divided by 1/4 multiplied by 10).

9. **79.** Each of the twelve ways to make a quarter can be paired off with one another once, including itself. So 12 + 11 + 10...+ 1 = 78. The only other possibility not included in the twelve is 5 dimes.

10. **500,500.** Pairing up the numbers makes 499 pairs, each totaling a thousand, for 499,000. Add the one 1000 that is unpaired. That's 500 thousands plus the 500, which was unpaired.

11. **18 years old.**

12. **0.36 seconds.** An hour has 3600 seconds, so 1% is 36 seconds. 1/100 of that is 36/100 or 0.36.

13. **0.028 meters.** To quadruple something, the additional portion must represent 3 parts so when added to the original, you have 4 parts. .021 divided in thirds is .007. Multiply it by the 4 parts to find .028 meters.

14. **He was 10 1/2, and she was 3 1/2.** The key word is *was*. Guess-and-check then begins at 24 and goes downward from there. (This problem can also be solved by algebra, where D = M + 7 and M = D/3.)

15. **d.** There are two ways to solve this. Find the areas of the circles using the radius squared and multiplying by pi. For the 10-inch, the area is 25 pi while the 14-inch is 49 pi. Close to double. Another way to think about it: suppose the pizza came in 10-inch and 14-inch square boxes. The total area would be 10 x 10 (100) and 14 by 14 (196). Again, almost double the area.

16. **120.** For every set of 4 four-legged stools and 3 three-legged stools, he needs 25 legs. Thus, he can make 40 sets for a total of 120 three-legged stools and 160 four-legged stools.

17. **12.** The difference between 1/3 and 1/2 is 1/6. Since 6 problems represents 1/6 of the total problems, there must be 36 problems in all.

18. **1/3.** To find the number, multiply 4% by 25, which gives 100% (3 x 25 = 75, and 25/75 = 1/3).

19. **38.** Totaling the age differences from the youngest to oldest is 2 + 4 + 6 + 8 + 10 or 30 years. 198 – 30 = 168. Divide by 6 to find the youngest age of 28.

20. **6 7/8 miles.** The first person walks 1 1/2 miles every hour while the second walks 1 1/4 miles per hour. Together, they cover 2 3/4 miles each hour. Multiply this by the 2 1/2 hours and you have the distance.

21. **96%.** 24 doughnuts divided by 25 students is the same as 24/25. If you change this to the equivalent fraction, you get 96/100.

22. **16.66%.** If you change the percents to fractions, you have 1/10, 1/9, 1/8, 1/7, so converting 1/6 to a percent completes the pattern, since 20% is 1/5.

23. **b.** Assume that the item costs $100. Under case a, the item is reduced to $85 then reduced 15% more, or $12.75, to a total of $72.25. Under case b, the item costs $70.00.

24. **1/7.** The spinner would have 4 blues, 2 reds, and 1 white of the same size.

25. **A = 59, C = 1424.** The difference between the numbers is increasing by powers of 4. 4^2 is 16, 4^3 is 64 and 4^4 is 256. To find C, add 4^5 or 1024. The answer to B is 60, found by subtracting 4^1, or 4. A is 4^0 (or one) less than 60.

26. **A little over 8 minutes.** The Sun is approximately 93 million miles away. Divide that by 186,000 to find 500 seconds, or 8 minutes, 20 seconds.

27. **0.85.** The difference between the two end numbers is 1.0. Dividing this number into four parts gives 0.25, the difference between each pair of numbers. Starting with the first number, add 0.25 to each. As a check, the difference between C and the last number should be .25.

28. **1.03.** By comparing any two scales, you can calculate how much heavier a particular shape is compared to another. Use this information to solve the third balance. For example, compare the first two scales and the O is .13 heavier than the □. From the third scale, you know that O + .13 + □ = .69 so subtract .13 and divide in half to find □ = .28. Add .13 to find O = .41. Δ = .34. *OR* you could add up all 3 balances to find how much two of each shape weighs. Divide this by two to find the sum of the three shapes.

29. **500.** Pair up the 11.11 with the 88.88 and the 22.22 with the 77.77, and so on, to find 5 groups of 99.99.

30. **77.** Since 5 chickens and 2 cows have 18 legs total, we can divide the 198 into eleven sets, each having the 5 to 2 ratio. There are 55 chickens and 22 cows.

31. **$47.04.** The $9.60 represents the 2/7 not spent of the 5/7 given, or 10/49 of the total allowance. Divide by 10 to find 1/49 of the allowance, which is $0.96. The total is 49 times that.

32. **$4.50.** She had four dollar coins and a half dollar. She gave away $1.50.

33. **1 1/3.** Subtract the first bottom number from the second bottom number and then triple that difference to get the answer.

34. **32/120 or 4/15.** Breaking the day into twelve-minute pieces (5 each hour for 24 hours) gives 120 parts. He slept for 32 of these twelve-minute blocks.

35. **2,002,114.**

36. **190.** 1/5 of the students left at first and then later, thrice that, or 3/5, left. In between, 1/8 of the 4/5 (or 1/10 of the total) also left. Therefore, if 4/5 + 1/10 already left, then the last 1/10 must equal the 19 still eating.

37. **1 ÷ (2 ÷ 3) x 4 = 6.**

38. 400,000,000 quarters.

39. 4300. It takes 20 nines to write the numbers 0–99, so from 0 to 899, it takes 180. From 900 to 1000, it takes a nine in each of the numbers plus the same 20 it takes from 0 to 99. Thus, it takes 300 nines to write from 0 to 1000. So it also takes 300 to write the numbers from 1000 to 1999, which means that from 1000 to 8999, it takes 2700 nines. From 9000 to 9999 it takes 1000 (since each starts with 9) and the same 300 needed from 0 to 1000.

40. 499,999,999.5.

41. $2500. Ten million quarters means 1/4 of that in dollars, or $2,500,000. To find 1%, you divide by 100; so to find 1/10 of that, you can divide the total by 1000.

42. 1200. The lowest common denominator of 6, 8, and 10 is 120. Every 120th pizza has all three toppings.

43. 44 cars. They sold 32 basic and 12 deluxe. (8 x 6.50 + 3 x 9.50 = $80.50 so divide 322 by 80.5 to get 4 sets of 8 to 3 carwashes.)

44. 1 8/9, 2 4/9

45. ♣ = 2. ♦ = 12. ♥ = 16. Substitute the ♦ and the ♥ in the top balance. This makes ♣ + (♣ + 10) + (♣ + 14) = 30 or 3♣ + 24 = 30.

46. Yes, five times over. You would have 5 million dollars.

47. 8/9. The problem ends up being 2/3 divided by 3/4. Another way to look at it: 3/4 is 9 parts out of 12. Now, 2/3 is 8 out of the same 12. So 2/3 would cover 8/9 of the larger fraction. The whole equation can be written like this: 2/3 ÷ 3/4 = 2/3 x 4/3 = 8/9

48. 0.995. The difference of .09 can be broken into 18 parts of .005. This part can then be subtracted from the endpoint (.10 – .005 = .995) or added from the beginning point.

49. a. 600 x 200 ÷ 400 – 300 + 200 = 200.

b. 200 ÷ 300 x 600 – 400 + 200 = 200.

50. b. From scales 2 and 3, you can replace the θθ on scale 1 with ΔΔ □. Remove a Δ from both sides and you have O = □Δ; therefore, OO = O□Δ.

51. c. Since the scales are balanced, you can turn scale 2 around and then add it to scale 1. Subtracting the ♣ from both sides leaves the answer.

52. 6, 12, 14, 10.

53. 17 + 17 + 17 + 17 + 16 + 16 = 100.

54. 31. Father and son will always be 31 years apart, so Mr. Femiano must be 62.

55. 156 (13 x 12) and 195 (13 x 15). Make a chart of the multiples of 13.

56. 90. The 27 years represents 3/5 of Katrina's age, so 1/5 would be 9 and her full age would be 45 (45 x 2 = 90).

57. 54 x 3 = 162.

58. $1.50. (Each six-pack costs $4.50 for a total of $13.50). One way to solve this is to subtract the extra $9 and divide the remaining into 4 parts (a six-pack is now the same price as a single drink) to find the cost of one bottle.

59. 2.613. To generate an even sum you must have an even number of odd digits. Since the hundredths digit is odd, and the tenths digit must be even (as all doubles are), then only one other digit is odd, either in the ones or thousandths place. The tenths can be only 6 or 8, and the thousandths can be only 3 or 4. The only two answer choices where the ones are less than the thousandths are 3.814 and 2.613. And since the first two digits together must be evenly divisible by the last two digits together, then 3.814 doesn't work.

60. **9:23:00 A.M.** The temperature doubling has nothing to do with the problem. If the temperature increases 7/8 degrees every 3 minutes, 7.5 seconds, then every 8 such time periods will bring a temperature increase of 7 degrees (3 minutes, 7.5 seconds times 8 = 25 minutes). So, 52.5 degrees divided by 7 degrees equals 7 1/2 periods of 25 minutes, or 187 1/2 minutes. Even quicker: Divide 52.5 by 7/8 to find 60 periods of 3 minutes, 7.5 seconds each.

61. **15 miles.** The pattern is as follows: two sons cross the river, one stays, and the other returns. A dad rows over, and the son who is already over there rows back. This pattern continues until all dads and one son are across. The 15th trip is with the last two sons.

62. **9990.** The lowest common multiple of 10, 30, and 45 is 90. The multiple of 90 that is closest to 10,000 is 111 x 90.

63. **450.** From 0 to 99, there are 45 numbers where the tens is larger than the ones. So from 0 to 1000, there would be ten times that.

64. **101.** From 0 to 99 there are ten (0, 11, ... 99); thus from 0 to 999 there are ten times that, or 100. The number 1000 itself is the 101st.

65. **1.** The progression decreases by an increasing divisor. Working backwards, you divide by 10^4, then 10^3, followed by 10^2. 10^1 (B = 1) and 10^0 are the next two.

66. **Each one weighs 225.** The total weight of the four people is 600 pounds. The total weight of the first two people is 150 pounds, leaving the 450 pounds to the remaining two people.

67. **24 kilometers.** The 2 to 5 ratio actually means 3/5 of the time is spent uphill and the other 40% is downhill. This means 12 hours uphill and 8 downhill.

68. **1 2/7.** Each □ equals 3/7. Or, □□□ represents 3/7 of the total shown (3/7 x 3).

69. **Odd.** Pair up the 0 and 50, 1 and 49 ... The median is 25, which has nothing to pair with and so makes the answer odd.

70. **6 out of 15, or 40%.** For every sweet-flavored gumball, 1 out of 5 is strawberry. Since there are twice as many sweets, there would be 10 sweets (2 strawberries) for every 5 sour. Since there are four times as many cherries as strawberies, there would be 2 strawberries in every 10 sweets. So, the chance of getting a strawberry is 2 in 15 with one dime and 3 times higher with 30¢.

71. **550 and 55.** Since one number is 10 times larger, there must be 11 parts to make the whole sum (605/11 =55).

72. **60 pounds.** Together they weigh 240%, or 2 2/5 times, the son. The son must weigh 5/12 (the inverse of 2 2/5) of 360, or 150 pounds. The dad weighs 210.

73. **1/2.** The height after the third bounce is 1/8 of the initial height. If the fraction is the same each time, then 1/8 must equal three times some number. That number is 1/2 (1/2 x 1/2 x 1/2 = 1/8).

74. **$22 more than Jane and $38 more than Gia.** Let's say that Julie started out with $50. Since she gave away $10, Julie had $40 left. After the money is

distributed, Julie still has $10 more than Jane, so Jane must now have $30. Since Julie still has $20 more than Gia, Gia must now have $20. But Jane gave $8 of her $10 to Gia, so her pre-transaction total was $28 ($30 – $2). And since Gia got $8 from Jane, her pre-transaction total was $12 ($20 – $8). If Julie had $50 to start with, then she had $22 more than Jane ($50 – $28) and $38 more than Gia ($50 – $12).

75. **□.** In the fourth row, Δ = 2 1/2 . Thus in the third row, □ = 1 5/6. Using this, you can find that □ = 5 1/6 in the second row. The fifth row shows that ⊗ = 3 5/6.

76. **0.15 kg.** The relative weight of a box and books together: 5 1/2 parts (1 part box, 4 1/2 parts books). Since 1.1 kg is the weight of *two identical boxes*, then 0.55 (the weight of one box) divided by 5.5 (the number of parts in one set of box and books) = 0.1. So the 3 books weigh .45 kg (4.5 x .1), or .15 kg each.

77. **27.** She is on rung 14 at the beginning, and she ends up on rung 18. Going from midway to 2/3 of the way gives you 1/6 of the total. From midway to the top is 4 1/2 steps. Multiply this by 6 parts to find the total.

78. **5050.** Notice the hearts on the bottom line of each drawing. First there is one, then two and so on. Therefore, in the 100th drawing, there would be 1 at top and 100 on the bottom layer. So this problem becomes the sum of 1 to 100. Pair up the 1 and 99 ... to find 49 pairs of 100 plus the 100th row. This equals 5000. Add in the unpaired 50 to make 5050.

79. **65%.** 84 x 20 = 1680. 85 x 19 = 1615, so the other score must be 65.

80. **Win.** However, your chances of winning are only 2/15. There are fifteen possible outcomes (0 + 1, 0 + 2 ... 4 + 5) with only 2 wins (1 + 2, 0 + 3). For every 15 tries ($15), you win twice ($14).

81. **82¢.** The teacher has two of each coin.

82. **-0.6.** The numbers are –0.8 and –0.2.

83. **3/4.** The numbers are 1 1/2 and 1/2.

84. **498.** It takes one increase to make the second number, two increases to make the third number, etc.; so for the 101st number, it takes 100 increases of 5, or 500. Add the -2 to make 498.

85. **Row 166,667, Column D.** 1,000,000 divided by 6 = 166666.66. The 2/3 is a remainder of 4, which is Column D in the next row.

86. **Thursday, 3:30 p.m.** Every hour, they work at the rate of 1/36 + 1/28 of a one-coat job. This reduces to 4/63, so in 63 hours they will have four-coated it. Therefore, it will take 31 1/2 hours for them to complete the two coats. Another way to look at it: Since they work at 4/63 to one-coat, they'd need 126 parts to double-coat. 126 divided by 4 = 31 1/2 hours.

87. **0.081.** From the diagonal, determine H = .128. Then G = .420, so A can now be found and the remaining numbers can be filled in.

88. **160%.** Kerri has 5/8 of the money Ashley has. Ashley has 8/5 of the money Kerri has. 8/5 = 160%.

89. **888 + 88 + 8 + 8 + 8 and 555 + 55 (nine of them) + 5.**

90. **$47.43.** The 15% tip on top of the 10% tax becomes16 1/2% tax (since it would be 15% of 110% of the bill, which now includes tax), so the cost of the food + 10% + the 16 1/2% = food + 26 1/2%. Therefore, 126.5% of the bill is $60 (60 divided by 1.265 = 47.43).

91. **$62.** Working backwards, she ends with 0; so before ride five, she must have had $2. Before ride four, she had 6. Before ride three, she had 14. Before ride two, she had 30. Before the first ride, she had 62.

92. **13,501.** 0 + 999, 1 + 998...499 + 500. The sum of the digits in all of these pairs is 27. So, 50 pairs x 27 = 13,500. Adding the digits in 1000 completes the problem.

93. **Dom pays $10 and Craig pays $6.** The friend paid $1 for each of the 8 dishes he shared. All 8 dishes cost $24 total.

94. **1lb. 1oz.** Suppose he pays $1 per pound for the seed. He wants to sell a 10-pound bag for $17.00, but he actually sells the ten pounds for $16.00. 170/160 = 1 1/16. In other words, every time he thinks he sold 16 pounds, he actually sold 17 for the price of 16.

95. **72.** There are 12 (4 x 3) routes from Jonesville to Clarksville. There are 12 routes from Clarksville to Jonesville, but he can't repeat a route on the return trip. Since there are 3 routes from Clarksville to Thomasville and 4 routes from Thomasville to Jonesille, multiply 12 x (3 + 4), which is 12 x 7 = 84. Then also subtract the 12 repeated routes (84 - 12 = 72).

96. **c.** From scale 2, we know OO = Δ□. Going to scale 1 and substituting, we find □□ = Δ□O. Subtract □ and you find □ = ΔO. Substitute ΔO for each □ in scale 1 and you find ΔΔ = O. Substitute this in scale 3 to find OOO is the same as □□, as shown in scale 1.

97. **5.** Write the bottom two numbers as a fraction. The top number represents the percent.

98. **7 inches.** One way to do it is to find the diagonal length of the whole cube, from corner to opposite corner, then divide this in half. The cube measures 8 by 8 by 8. So, the diagonal of the bottom face can be found using the Pythagorean formula (square root of the sum of 8 squared plus 8 squared. [square root of 128]). Now, use this line to make one side of a new right triangle, whose other side is the full height of 8 inches. The hypotenuse of this triangle is the diagonal of the cube. The square root of 194 is close to the square root of 196, which is 14. Cut this in half, since its midpoint is the cubes' center.

99. **$17.** The $28 represents 140%, so divide 2800 by 140 and get $20, the cost before the 40%. 85% of $20 is $17.

100. **Movie B.** It had an average attendance of 393 per show; Movie A averaged 381.

101. **65π or a little over 204 miles.** With the 5-foot diameter, it travels 5π each revolution. Multiply this by 1320 for distance per minute. Multiply by 60 for the hourly speed. Divide by the distance in a mile. Note that 1320 is 1/4 of 5280.

102. **67 1/2%.** The women started with 40%, then together bought 12 1/2% and 15%.

103. **120.** 75% of 88 is 66. 66 ÷ .55 (55%) = 120.

104. **5 cubed or 125 cubes.** The smaller cube has faces of 25 square centimeters, making it a 5-by-5-by-5 cube. The larger cube is 25-by-25-by-25. Thus you can fit 5 smaller cubes across the length, width, and height of the larger cube.

105. **67.** A repeating pattern emerges of odd, odd, even. Thus, 2/3 of the numbers will be odd (from 1 to 99), plus the last number will be odd because it is next in the pattern.

